Ted Aistrope
5808 - 105A ave.

Christmas 1973.
aunt Iva

# all colour book of Horses

## by Elizabeth Johnson

Octopus Books

# Contents

First Published in 1972 by
Octopus Books Limited
59 Grosvenor Street, London W1

ISBN 7064 0070 4
© Octopus Books Limited

Produced by Mandarin Publishers Limited
Printed in Hong Kong

# Horses in the Past

Although the colourful history of the horse as we know it today only stretches back as far as the history of man, we know that a small animal, Eohippus, existed fifty million years ago. Over the ages this small animal, approximately the size of a fox has evolved until it has developed into Equus as we now know it. Man's first encounters with the horse have been revealed by the discovery of cave paintings depicting the horse as a hunted creature. Time passed and gradually man found more uses for the horse than just as a source of food. He learnt that the horse could be harnessed for work, and he could be ridden enabling man to cover much greater distances. The relationship between man and his horse is founded on a mutual trust and respect and the comradeship between the two species has survived the tumult of countless wars and disasters and the inevitable indignities of a servant-master relationship. The horse has remained steadfast and loyal over thousands of years but he has never lost his personality or individual characteristics that make him such a fascinating and noble beast.

Today the horse is considered mainly as a source of pleasure and is the companion of man in many different spheres, but it is only comparatively recently that the horse as a worker has disappeared from our everyday life. Even now, as you read through the following chapters, you will realize that he still has a job to do in many parts of the world where no machine could ever replace him. It is hard to believe that horses were used in war as recently as the Second World War. It is easier to remember them further back in history, connected with such episodes as the American Civil War and the Crimea, or William the Conqueror and even further back during the great Greek and Roman civilizations. As the only means of transport on land before the invention of the internal combustion engine and steam propelled vehicles, the horse was unrivalled by any other animal, and played an extremely important part in men's lives. Interest in breeding was developed very early, and his horse was often a man's most valued possession. Always willing and eager to serve, the horse holds a unique position in man's history, and it is important to recognize the contribution made by this most faithful of servants.

Over the ages the horse has been honoured and remembered by man. Statues and paintings abound in every corner of the earth where the horse has been part of life, and he is a principal figure on the stage of mythology. The Greeks were especially fond of deifying horses, they drew the sun god's chariot, and Pegasus the winged horse is a well-known figure in their mythology. No other animal has been similarly treated throughout the ages of man because no other creature has ever been so useful or given itself so entirely to the service of the human race. Together with the dog and the cat, the horse has been closer to man than any other member of the animal kingdom, but the horse has been held in far greater respect due to his vital importance in mens' lives before mechanized travel and due to his strength and power. Man has made the horse his servant, but one always experiences the feeling when dealing with a horse that he is doing what is required of him because *he* wants to and not because the master wishes it. It is in the horse's nature to serve but never to become the slave of the human race. With a toss of his head or a sudden quick movement he can make a fool of us if he so desires. When he no longer wants someone on his back, he lets him know in no uncertain manner, and in a second the rider is sitting on the ground far removed from his lofty position. When this is done for the sheer fun of it, you can almost imagine the horse looking condescendingly down at you and saying 'Just so long as we both know who is really the boss'.

Contact with horses can teach the human race much that is worth knowing. Patience is an essential ingredient in any horse-man relationship, as are tolerance and perseverance. Calmness and quietness are also essential, since the horse is a highly sensitive creature and basically frightened of sudden assaults on his peace and tranquillity. Animals that are destined to spend their lives in noisy surroundings, such as police horses and the ceremonial mounts of cavalry soldiers, undergo a long and arduous training period to acquaint them with all types of disturbance and noise. But for the most part horses that are kept purely for pleasure live uncomplicated, peaceful lives which is the least we can offer for the deprivation of their freedom.

**Previous page: Left** Some of the most highly trained animals in the world are rodeo horses, and the sport arose out of the everyday work of the cowboys on the ranches. This is an early painting of a North American cowboy roping cattle in the wild west of North America.

**Right** The Chinese have perpetuated the memory of their animals by making exquisite china and porcelain models of many of them. This Chinese horse, complete with its saddle and regalia, now resides in the Victoria and Albert Museum in London – many thousands of miles from its original home in the Far East.

---

**Top left** In all the great cities of the world there are many fine equestrian statues commemorating figures in history mounted on their chargers. This is a statue in Paris of Joan of Arc astride her magnificent horse, and she was reputedly a brilliant horsewoman able to handle animals only considered suitable for men.

**Bottom left** The Greeks were great horsemen and many illustrations of their riding activities survive to this day. The horsemen shown on the side of this Greek vase are riding their spirited stallions in a race, and are riding bareback, as saddles had not been invented. The vase could have been given as a prize for the winner of the race.

**Top right** A screen painting by an eighteenth century Japanese artist of a twelfth century general in full battle regalia at the Battle of the Uji River 1184.

**Bottom right** A relief of the Roman Imperial Period, very probably a representation of Alexander the Great, one of the great figures in Greek history. Alexander the Great was the son of the King of Macedonia in Northern Greece, and from an early age he showed a great sympathy in his handling of horses and perhaps one of the most famous stories to be associated with this great warrior involves his charger, Bucephalus. Alexander acquired this magnificent black steed when he was a mere boy of thirteen, the horse was declared unrideable but the young Alexander was able to win the horse's confidence and used him for many years on his arduous and lengthy campaigns.

**Above** One of the beautiful horses which form part of the fountain in the Residenzplatz in Salzburg; and **left** the bronze horses of St Mark's, Venice dating from the thirteenth century.

**Right** The last remaining link with the past is thought to be *Equus Przevalski*. Przevalsky's horse still roams wild on the plains of Mongolia and many more can be seen in zoos all over the world. The colour of these horses is predominantly dun, red dun and brown dun with the characteristic mealy nose and eyes. Another strange feature is the upright growth of their spiky manes.

# Foals

When a favourite mare has fulfilled her purpose as a riding and working animal, nothing brings more pleasure than to breed from her. The sight of a new-born foal playing happily in one's own paddock can bring endless fun and pride both to the owner and the mare. Foals are amongst the most independent of any young animals and two or three days after birth they are sure to be found investigating all sorts of strange objects and exploring new places alone. They are born comics and will provide rewarding and amusing results for anyone equipped with a camera.

The breeding of a foal can be a most rewarding as well as time-consuming experience. Often if a mare sustains an injury which renders her useless for ridden work the answer is to put her into foal. Choosing a suitable stallion can be difficult but the Hunters Improvement Society has done a tremendous amount of work through their Premium Scheme to encourage the use of a quality stallion at a reasonable stud fee.

The mare will carry her foal for eleven months before birth and within minutes after it is born the foal will attempt to get to its feet and take its first wobbly, unsteady steps. Somehow there always seems to be far too much leg for the foal to cope

with during the first few hours and he will frequently fall over his own ungainly legs. However, he rapidly learns how to get them under control and is soon leaping around the paddock with all the gay abandon of any young animal in a new world. Mares and foals are often all turned out together in order to encourage the youngsters to play with each other and develop their limbs by racing round the field. It is a legacy from the days when horses were subject to the dangers of predatory animals that enables the young foal to become mobile in such a short space of time. When part of a herd of wild ponies, it was essential that both mare and foal should be able to move off with the herd as soon as danger threatened.

The countless wild native ponies of Britain foal quite naturally on the wide open expanse of their native Exmoor and Dartmoor, or in the New Forest, as do the wild horses of Wyoming in North America, but the more valuable thoroughbred mares and breeding stock are kept under constant watch on the stud farms. Some establishments even have close circuit television to keep an eye on their mares throughout the night. Mares are very sensitive about foaling in the presence of human beings and some will refuse to foal unless left completely alone.

**Previous page: Left** A rest in the sun.
**Right** A roan pony and her palomino
foal seemingly ripe for mischief. Roans
are ponies that have white hairs mixed
fairly evenly with hairs of another
colour – bay, black or chestnut, and
the coat often has a blueish tinge to it.
Palominos are always pale gold in
colour with a white mane and tail, and
neither of these colourings constitute a
breed in themselves.

**Below** Two very young foals, one
Arab and one Thoroughbred with their
mothers on a stud farm. They are put
out in the same field so that they will
give each other plenty of exercise. For
the first few days, however, foals find
their legs much too long and very
difficult to control, and they stick extremely close to their mothers. Then,
as their confidence grows, they begin
to explore their field and make friends.
The chestnut Thoroughbred foal makes
the first advances and after a little

difficulty wins the confidence of the shy
and delicate Arab. Thereafter the two
are inseparable . . . . . though it is stil
the chestnut which takes the lead.

**Right** Mares and foals . . . a Thorough
bred mare and her foal, which has beer
broken to halter. Youngsters are usually
broken in between the ages of three and
five years and are considered to be
foals up to the January following thei
birth – about nine months.

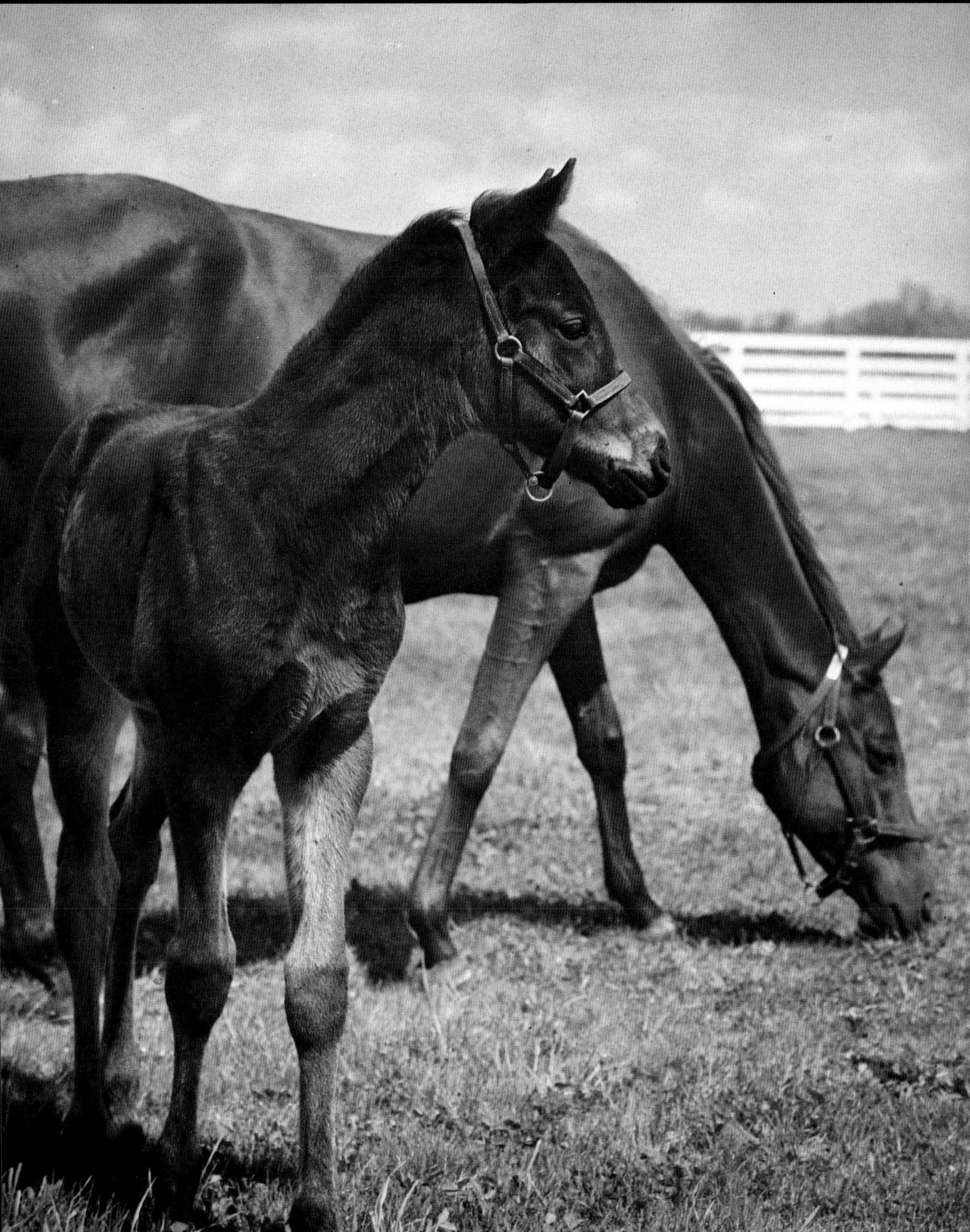

**Left** The Shire horse is essentially a heavily built, working horse and this foal has travelled to a show with his mother. The bustle and hurry of a big show is obviously all too much for this little chap and he has settled himself next to the horsebox for a quick nap.

**Right** A New Forest pony foal has a good scratch. At this age this presents no problem, but as he grows older he will not find it quite so easy. Fences, gates, branches and often humans are considered ideal scratching posts by horses, and they will practically knock you over as they rub up and down in the small of your back

**Below** A young New Forest pony foal only a few hours old. He has not yet got on to his legs.

**Left** Highlands are handsome stocky ponies and were much esteemed by Queen Victoria for their endurance and reliability in carrying stags across the deer forests of Scotland. They make excellent pack ponies and also go well in harness classes. This attractive creamy colouring with black mane and tails is called dun, and often the ponies have a black dorsal stripe and black stockings.

**Below and top right** Hardly foals any more . . . . these three foals are really bored with the proceedings at a local show although they have all won prizes.

However, two of them can at least commiserate with each other, but the third just looks plain miserable.

**Bottom right** Two Shetland pony foals at a show. Shetlands are probably the oldest and hardiest of Britain's native breeds and rarely grow much above three feet even when living on good grass in the south as opposed to the sparse grazing and hard climate of their native islands. Their popularity grows continually and there are now three types of Shetland bred in America; for riding, for draught events and for driving.

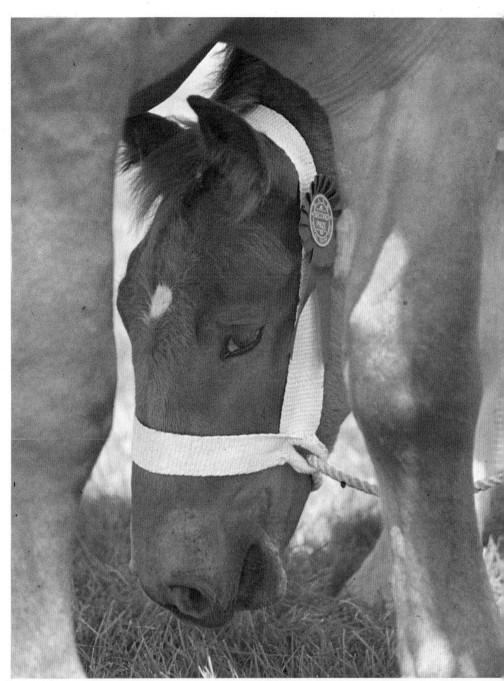

**Below** In natural conditions foals will continue to feed from their mothers until such time as her milk dries up. In artificial conditions created by man, a foal can be weaned at any time after four and a half months. A two week old foal will begin to nibble at the grass and as soon as this is noticed attempts can be made to encourage the foal to eat concentrates.

**Right** For many people, the Arab epitomises the horse in all its glory. The proud bearing and presence of the Arab is unmistakeable and it is from three great Arabian horses, the Darley Arabian, the Godolphin Barb and the Byerley Turk that the Thoroughbred sprang. Renowned for its stamina, beauty, soundness and speed, the Arab remains one of the purest of the equine breeds. This beautiful Arab mare has clearly produced a foal worthy of its proud ancestry.

# Show jumping

Show jumping today is a very popular sport both in the United States and Europe and interest is growing increasingly in South Africa, Canada and Australia. In England the heroes and heroines of international arenas are known to most people, and the more famous of their horses have huge numbers of fans. In the last fifteen years television has been responsible for turning the riders and their horses into stars and for the interest taken in the many different shows all over the world which culminate in the four-yearly Olympics; but it was the members of the BSJA in the years immediately after the war that were responsible for building up the British team to a standard comparable with that of the continental teams so that their successes aroused the interest of the general public. The names of the fifties are still as well-known as those of today:—Colonel Sir Mike Ansell, who was the leading light of the BSJA and organizer of the Royal International Horse Show at the White City in 1947, of the Horse of the Year Show at Harringay and also the British team's excellence abroad; Colonel Harry Llewellyn and the great Foxhunter who are show jumping's heroes, Pat Smythe with Prince Hal and Tosca, Peter Robeson and Craven A, and Wilf White and Nizefela.

Since then the numbers of riders and of shows, both national and international have grown considerably. Douglas Bunn started the All-England Jumping Ground at Hickstead in 1960 which now rivals the great continental show grounds like Aachen, Hamburg and Rotterdam. Many more women are now among the stars and they have their own World and European Championships and the coveted Queen Elizabeth II Cup at the Royal International Horse Show, which is as prized as the King George V Cup for men. Alison Westwood and The Maverick, Anneli Drummond-Hay and Merely-a-Monarch, Marion Mould and the amazing pony, Stroller, and recently Anne Moore and Psalm have all made show jumping the exciting, dramatic and popular sport that it is now. With Alan Oliver, who is still jumping successfully after twenty years, Harvey Smith and David Broome, European Champion three times running, and newcomers like Michael Saywell, Britain has a large number of top class riders, from which to select representatives for the 1972 Olympics at Munich.

In the United States the team was reorganized after the war under the successive captaincies of Colonel John Woffard, Arthur MacCashin and Bill Steinkraus who took over in 1955 and was individual Gold Medallist on Snowbound at the Mexico Olympics in 1968. The team has been a formidable one for many years and one which has been reckoned as the most stylish in the world—principally from the time that Bertalan de Nemethy was appointed trainer just before the Stockholm Olympics. Since then their team has done consistently well in Nations Cups and individual events in Europe and England as well as America and has won the President's Cup twice since its inauguration in 1965. The three important shows are at New York, Harrisburg and Toronto, together with the Pan American Games.

The European countries have produced famous riders, horses and teams consistently, many of whom have been winning for the last twenty years. Hans Winkler from Germany and his courageous little mare Halla are always remembered for their remarkable performance at the Stockholm Olympics, when Winkler had injured himself before the final round and went into jump barely able to stay in the saddle because of the pain. Halla virtually took herself around the enormous course and had a clear round to win both the individual Gold Medal and the Team Gold for Germany. Pierre Jonqueres d'Oriola from France with various horses such as Ali Baba, Lutteur and Pomona has been winning since 1947, the d'Inzeo brothers from Italy have between them over the last two decades won every major honour several times over, and Nelson Pessoa, the great Brazilian show jumper and his famous horse Gran Geste are all among the celebrated members of this sport.

In 1958 the first and only team from South Africa came to Europe and competed successfully, but since about 1960 the horse sickness ban has been in force and prevented riders from South Africa from bringing their own horses or competing in teams outside their own country. However, South African riders have come to Europe and Bob Grayston,

Mickey Louw and Gonda Butters are well-known outside their own country. In 1970 the indoor show at Johannesburg had a world class touch as Broome, Pessoa, d'Oriola and Schridde all went over to compete against the locals. In Australia and New Zealand there is a lively interest, though the teams are limited by the enormous distances they have to travel to compete against anyone else other than each other. In the year of the Tokyo Olympics however, the Australians had a grand tour of Europe after the games during their quarantine period, and they also sent a team to the Mexico Olympics. 1972 will see most of these riders in training for the Munich Olympics.

Some of the world's top show jumpers change hands for very considerable sums of money so it is not hard to imagine how such a valuable charge is cared for. But to reach this class it has not always been easy for horse and rider. Much hard work goes on behind the scenes before a top class jumper or eventer is produced. And it is the same for the show horses — ponies, hacks, hackneys and hunters — all have to undergo a thorough training period before they are ready to appear in the arena. The road is long and hard but the rewards at the top are worth every minute of the battle to get there. The feeling of pride as the champion rosette is pinned to your horse's bridle, and your lap of honour is applauded by the admiring crowd seems to make the work and effort all worthwhile. But it is not only the winning that counts, and it is just as pleasing to many people to produce a horse capable of going well in the hunting field or across country. A great deal of personal satisfaction can be gained by the good performance of your horse as a result of patient work beforehand whether he wins or not. It is extremely rare for the experience of working and living with horses to be unrewarding and they are capable of deep friendships and trust as well as great things in the arena. There are many dedicated workers behind the international show jumping scene who never appear in front of the television cameras but without whom no show jumper could exist. A great deal of work is involved in the keeping of valuable animals that work hard, and a professional rider does not have the time to do the half of it, so it is the grooms and people backstage as well as the riders and their horses who are responsible for the thrills of an international competition.

**Previous page: Left** The international and Olympic record of Hans Winkler, the mainstay of the German show jumping team for over twenty years, is unequalled. Individual Gold Medal winner, and three times team Gold Medallist at the Olympics, he has also won the World Show Jumping Championship twice, and the European Championships twice. This picture shows him riding Torphy in the Nations' Cup.

**Right** Captain of the USA show jumping team, and one of the prime architects of the American team's rise to prominence, Bill Steinkraus is an old campaigner in the show jumping ring. He won the individual Gold Medal at the Olympics in Mexico in 1968 on Snowbound. He is riding Fleet Apple, here, in the Nations Cup at Hickstead in 1971.

---

**Top left** There could hardly be two horses more different than Stroller and Merely-a-Monarch, but both have that indefinable star quality that attracts vast crowds to see them jump. Anneli Drummond-Hay and Monarch began their career in three day eventing and have won both the Badminton and Burghley horse trials. They later switched to show jumping. Anneli achieved her ambition to win the coveted Queen Elizabeth II Cup at the Royal International Horse Show on Monarch in 1970. Sadly Monarch had a very short season in 1971. Here he is jumping at Hickstead in 1970.

**Bottom left** Anneli Drummond-Hay riding Sporting Ford at Hickstead 1971. Her beautiful style of riding is clear for all to see and her horses are impeccably schooled and capable of performing in the dressage arena. She achieved a great double in 1969 when she won both the Hickstead Derby and the equivalent in Rome. This time her success was achieved on her bouncy ex-hunt servant's horse, Xanthos. European Ladies Champion in 1968, Anneli has proved her ability as a top lady rider and is possibily the most stylish of them all.

**Right** When Marion Coaks (now Mrs. Mould) graduated into adult show jumping she persuaded her father to let her keep her pony to use in adult classes. The phenomenal Stroller has proved his owner right in no uncertain way. Olympic individual Silver Medal winner, Stroller has a fantastic record both at home and abroad.

**Left** The reigning World Champion, David Broome. He has twice won an individual Bronze Medal at the Olympics and he has a style of riding which is a joy to watch. Three times European Champion he is one of the mainstays of the British show jumping team. Coming from Wales, David has always had a string of first class ponies and horses with which he has been incredibly successful. He won the World Championship riding Beethoven, one of the most difficult horses to manage within the confines of a show jumping arena. Here he is riding Manhattan.

**Right** Mary Chapot on White Lightening jumping at Hickstead in 1968, the year they won the Queen Elizabeth II Cup at the Royal International Horse Show. Later that year she took the place of Steinkraus in the American team at the Mexico Olympics as his horse Snowbound had lamed himself in the Individual event.

**Below** Nelson Pessoa, the brilliant Brazilian rider, has had to campaign in Europe as the lone representative of his country. He bases himself in Chantilly and competes regularly all over the continent. He has won the marathon Hickstead Derby on two occasions on his brilliant little grey, Gran Geste. He also won the men's European Show Jumping Championship at Lucerne in 1966. He has the enviable and possibly unrepeatable record of having won the gigantic Hamburg Derby on no less than four occasions on Gran Geste.

**Above** A splendid grey Irish horse and his rider take a drop fence in their stride. A cross country course will contain an enormous variety of fences, built up and down hill to test the stamina, skill and courage of both horse and rider.

**Left** A real horse-laugh from a famous horse obviously pleased with his victory at the Badminton Horse Trials in the spring of 1971. Ridden by Lt Mark Phillips, he is a potential member of the British Olympic Three Day Event team for 1972. Horses will often pull similar faces when they smell something unpleasant or alien, or if they are given something unusual to eat.

**Right** The final phase of a Three Day Event is the show jumping. This is to prove that after the rigours of the previous day's speed and endurance test and cross country course, the horse is still obedient and supple enough to complete a show jumping course. Princess Anne and her horse Doublet have done extremely well in the world of eventing. At the Badminton Horse trials in 1971 she finished fifth at her first attempt and then later in the season she won the Individual European Championship at the Burghley Horse Trials. Doublet was bred by the Queen and has been entirely produced by Princess Anne and her trainer Alison Oliver.

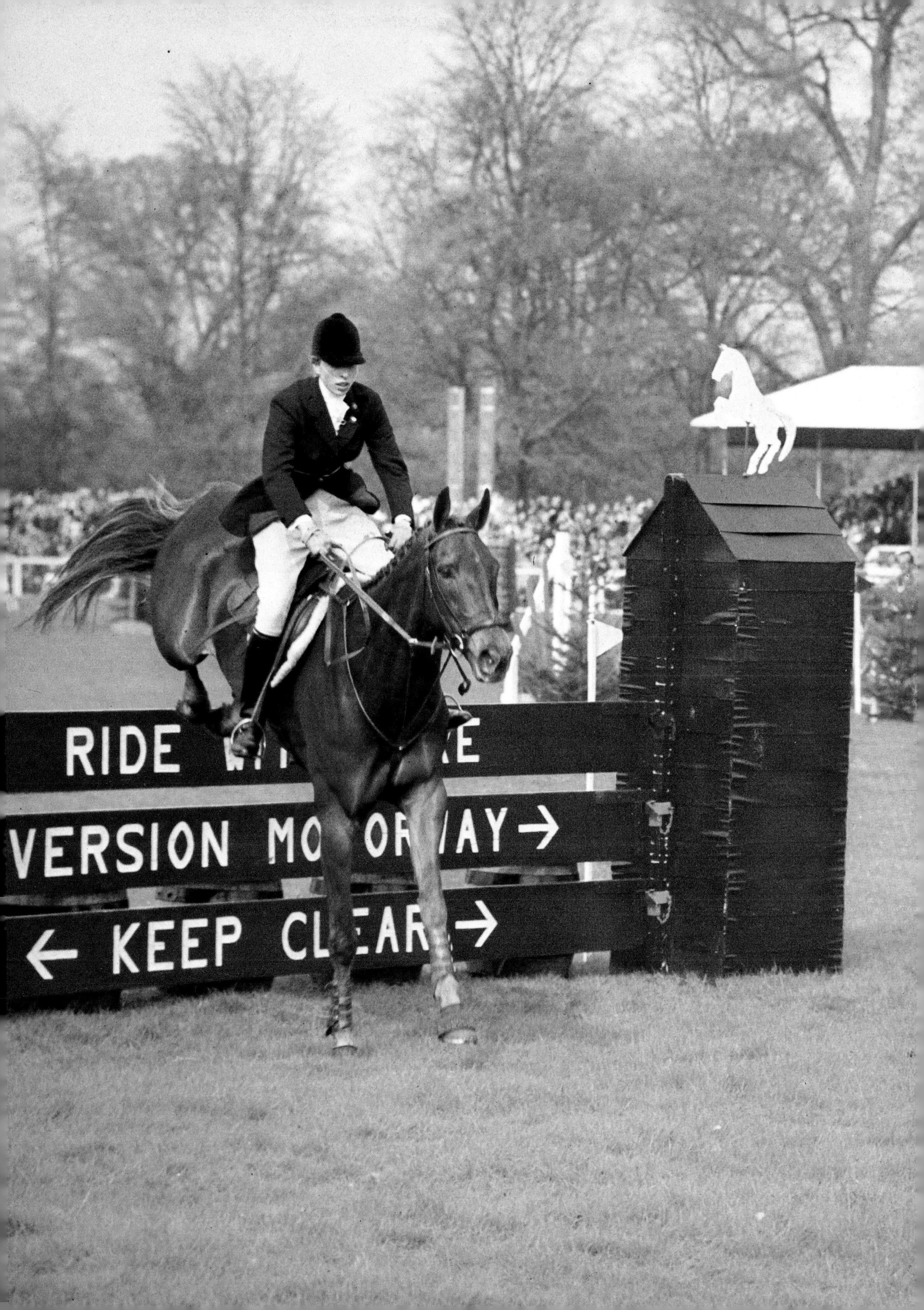
RIDE
VERSION
← KEEP

# Horses at Work and at Rest

Although in the present mechanized age working horses no longer form part of the everyday scene, there are areas of the world where horses are used to do certain jobs which no machine can do. Whatever the horse is doing, be it helping drive cattle in America or sheep in Australia; pulling a heavy load of timber through the Canadian forests; dragging the prize of deer from the hill in Scotland or helping to control unruly crowds as part of a police force, he gives his service willingly and without complaint. What is more he is reliable and works happily on provided he is well kept and well fed. He demands very little and gives his all in return.

Over the centuries the horse has been the major method of transport and communication until he was replaced by the internal combustion engine. Think of the Pony Express where letters were carried 1,900 miles in 8 days across the American continent, or the mail coaches of eighteenth and early nineteenth century England, which were famous for their speed and reliability. Not only mail, but passengers would also travel by this method.

At the end of the nineteenth century there were some 300,000 horses working for their living in the London area, 15,000 of them acting as cab and carriage horses while the rest pulled trams, coal carts, brewers' drays, greengrocers' carts, railway vans and many others. Nowadays the horse population of London is approximately 5,000, the majority being kept for the pleasure of riding although included in this figure are police horses, costermonger ponies and ceremonial horses.

Police horses are found the world over and are quite indispensible in some situations when no machine could do their job, such as when massed crowds need to be kept under control. They frequently give displays of their skill and training in public and demonstrate their acceptance of all sorts of frightening influences and ability to do things totally alien to them like jumping through or over flaming objects.

Although the heavy working horse has disappeared from the agricultural scene in Britain as a method of pulling farm machines, except on a very few isolated farms in northern England, these huge creatures can still be seen at the bigger agricultural shows, pulling brewers' drays, and, of course, at the Horse of the Year Show in London there is the magnificent sight of the six teams of heavy horses harrowing the arena during their majestic musical drive. Horses belonging to one brewery in London still work for their living delivering an average of 10,000 tons of beer a year within a three mile radius of their brewery.

Many thousands of horses all over the world also work for their living by providing riding lessons for those not lucky enough to have their own horse or pony. Countless riding schools and trekking centres cater for the needs of everybody wishing to ride, from the beginner to the more advanced pupil. Next time you go to your own riding school, just spare a thought for your hard-working mount, who has probably already done two or three hours work with the promise of more to come. As he patiently carries you round and round the school or sets off on his all-too-familiar hour-long hack, remember how much pleasure he can give you and reward him by trying to become a thoughtful and patient rider. Look after his needs when you have finished with him, don't just leave him standing in the yard and hope that someone will cope. They probably will, but how much nicer for you to show your appreciation by slackening off his girths and making him comfortable. One of the first rules to be learnt is to put your horse before yourself in all things.

This really is no hardship, since to be in the company of either horses or ponies can be the most relaxing of pastimes, whether you are riding quietly through the countryside, grooming energetically or just hanging over the stable door watching your favourite munch his way happily through his evening feed. Horses and ponies will not be hustled and hurried, they take life at their own speed and you cannot help becoming part of the relaxed happy atmosphere if you spend any time at all with them. Like dogs, every horse has its own distinctive character. Many of them are capable of strong attachment to their owners and have a good sense of humour and a strong sense of fun, which manifests itself in all sorts of ways.

If after a strenuous two or three days at a show, a horse is turned out in his own familiar paddock, he will invariably show his pleasure by

showing off for a few minutes, squealing, bucking and rolling before settling down to graze peacefully. Horses are gregarious and pine if they do not have a companion. Although they may graze at opposite ends of their field, they nevertheless appreciate the company. All sorts of habits and vices can develop when a horse becomes bored with its own company, and many horses will develop odd little tricks to amuse themselves, and you too if you are able to watch them for long enough. Some horses soon learn to untie ropes with amazing ease and a clip and chain can be the only answer if you are to be sure of keeping your horse in one place for more than five minutes. Horses have been known to remove their stable companions' head collars, and, if given the chance, systematically remove every article of grooming kit from a box and proceed to deposit each one on the stable floor. Buckets can also be

irresistible playthings when left lying around empty in the field.

Many horses soon learn how to undo the bolts on the stable door and realize that the answer is instant freedom. The first time this happens, it is usually just by chance, after the horse has been playing noisily with the bolt, enjoying the rattling noise. Safely shut in again, after a delicious spell of absolute freedom, it does not take the horse long to put two and two together and realize that playing with the bolt resulted in freedom. A safety clip on the bolt puts a stop to his little game.

Horses are described as vegetarians, and in the main they stick firmly to this rule. But, as with all rules, there are exceptions. A taste in buttons has been known — one particular horse could not resist coat buttons within his reach, and many horses enjoy stealing clothing or anything else that takes their fancy and prance off with their prize,

delighting to tease the owner by dashing off every time he comes near and attempts to retrieve it.

When the mood takes a horse, even the smallest scrap of paper fluttering in the hedge is an excuse for a display of fun and games. Many horses will play the fool to test the rider's reactions. On passing a certain spot on a familiar ride, your horse may shy sideways as if a herd of elephants was about to emerge from behind the nearest tree. But this is the same tree that you have been passing for months and surely there is nothing different? To your horse, who by this time resembles the fiery steed of mediaeval paintings with his distended nostrils, arched neck and high tail carriage, something is decidedly different. There is no logical explanation except that this is a sensitive animal with a mind of his own and it is possible that he sees things which we cannot see or understand.

Previous page: **Right** Horses in
Canada and Australia are still used fairly
frequently to haul timber down from
the great forests. The heavy collar
helps the working horse to take most
of the strain on his strong shoulders.
The market for English heavy horses
has widened recently due to the demand from parts of North America.

**Left** This unusually marked horse is an
Appaloosa. The name is derived from
the Palouse area in Idaho, home
of the Nez Perce Indians. Some
specimens are brilliantly and
strikingly spotted black on grey all
over. They also made some of the best
working ponies possessing particularly
good 'cow sense'. Although the tribe

was wiped out in battle the horses survived and have become one of the most popular breeds in America. This one is being trained in the corral of a big ranch to be obedient and accurate at speed.

**Right** In some parts of England and Scotland horses are still used for ploughing every day on small hill farms, and the competitions for ploughing with teams are becoming increasingly popular at agricultural shows. This pair are competing at the Southern Counties Agricultural Show.

**Below** An Australian farmer watches some of his sheep from his vantage point in the saddle. In this vast country the stockmen prefer to use horses for mustering their flocks and looking after their farms.

**Below** A guard dog at a show also acts as a companion to this chestnut show jumper. He has done his work for the day and is enjoying a hay net while his rider watches the rest of the competitions.

**Right** Horses are so built that they should eat little and often and thus they can happily spend most of the day grazing. This chestnut obviously thinks his bay companion is monopolizing a much tastier patch of grass!

**Left and below** A cow pony shows his ability to deal with unruly members of a beef herd. Although the Wild West is no more, the huge ranches of North America still rely on the skills of the modern cowboy and the agility and knowledge of his horses. No machine can do the job of this pair, as they sort the cattle out on a big beef ranch.

**Right** An Aboriginal stockman riding his stock horse in the Australian outback. Performing much the same function as the North American cowboy, the Aborigine is as happy when he is riding as he is on his own feet. In spite of his tendency to go 'walkabout' at any time, he makes a first-class stockman and has a definite understanding with the animals he is tending.

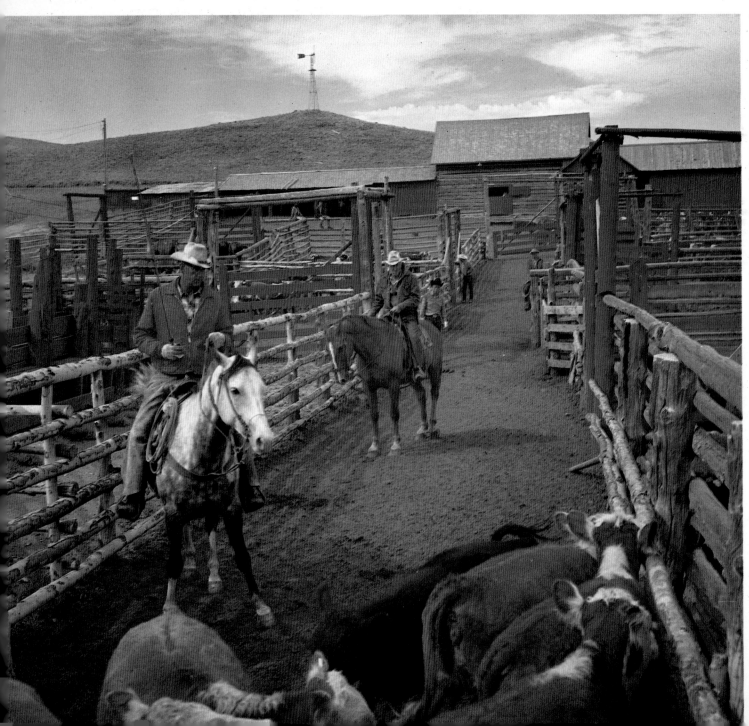

**Above** Naturally enough, horses have most fun playing with each other, and at the same time they will be doing themselves a lot of good. These Thoroughbred yearlings are gaining strength and stamina for their arduous careers as racehorses, and developing their gawky frames into the sleek muscular bodies capable of racing at high speeds on the track. They are from the Ocala Stud in Florida, a centre of Thoroughbred breeding which has come to the fore over the last twenty years in America.

**Left** Horses love having a good roll, particularly when they are hot after a hard day's work. Rolling seems to be infectious among horses, once one is down in the field, others follow suit. The old horse dealers used to say that a horse was worth another twenty guineas if he could roll right over from one side to the other.

**Right** A bay horse dozing in the shade on a hot summer's afternoon.

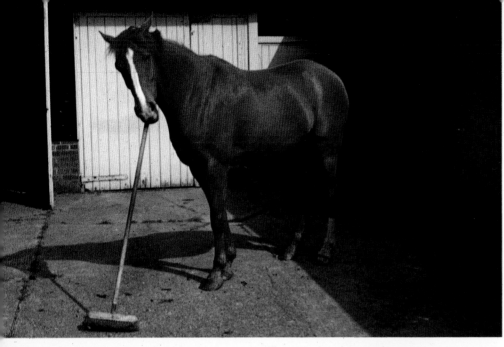

**Left** This horse, bred and owned by the author, has a tremendous sense of humour. One of his favourite pastimes if the broom is within reach is to swing the handle backwards and forwards between his front teeth, so that he looks as if he is sweeping his own yard.

**Below** A beautiful Palomino, given the freedom of his paddock, canters in perfect style with neck arched and head well tucked in.

**Right** Horses love companionship and on the whole make friends easily, though they can take strong dislikes and have to be separated. A broken horse that has to live alone is always very dependant on his owner and will be lonely without any company at all.

# Racing

'The sport of kings and the king of sports' — so the greatest of all forms of equine sport has been aptly described. As long as man is connected with horses he will always strive to prove that his horse is superior to that of his neighbour. The ultimate deciding factor must always be the speed and stamina of the respective horses. Since the earliest times, when speed was a necessity to escape from one's enemies, tremendous value has been placed on the ability to move faster than anybody else for very obvious reasons. Since the eighteenth century the specialized and selective breeding of Thoroughbreds has produced a succession of near perfect specimens of the horse, which have been capable of out-distancing all their rivals. In the history of racing on both sides of the Atlantic the names and records of Eclipse, St Simon and Hyperion in England and Sir Archy, Peytona, Fashion and Longfellow in America live on beside the names of today such as Kelso, the leading money winner in history, Nearco, Nijinsky and Mill Reef, to name just a few. Very few horses have unbeaten records but Ribot, the legendary Italian horse has this distinction. He won the Prix de l'Arc de Triomphe twice, and it is one of the most difficult races to win in the world. The fact that he managed this is a measure of his greatness.

The racing scene, whether it is Derby Day in England, Cup Day in Melbourne, the Durban July or the Kentucky Derby, attracts a colourful, noisy and essentially happy crowd of enthusiasts. Celebrities and the unknown public jostle noisily together around the parade paddock, assessing the chances of the runners, and many people (in particular the owners and trainers) know that vast sums of money are going to be won or lost in the next ten minutes. The bell rings and the jockeys mount to proceed down to the start. Starting stalls are now in use almost everywhere in the world and ensure the fairest possible beginning to any race. With a cry of 'They're off', the fluid blaze of colour sets out at a cracking pace. Excitement mounts as the horses separate, then the finishing post draws nearer and nearer, binoculars are trained on the leaders, the commentator engenders more excitement with every word and suddenly it is all over and the winner of yet another contest is led amidst the cheering crowds to the winner's enclosure. Proud owners and trainers make their way to congratulate horse and jockey. The lucky punters collect their winnings, the losers resolve never to trust their money to a four legged friend ever again, but sure enough they are the first to lay bets on the next race! The scene is the same the world over

wherever horses are produced to race against each other. Whether on the flat or over the sticks, the excitement is the same, from the local point-to-point to the Classics.

Many thousands of pounds can be won with a successful racehorse, but even more revenue can be secured when a successful horse is retired to stud. Other owners, all anxious to obtain some of the characteristics of a really top class horse, will pay vast sums for a nomination for their mares to the best stallion in the world. Yearlings such as Vaguely Noble and Crowned Prince then fetch record prices at the Yearling Sales purely on the merits of their breeding and the hoped-for racing results. Some of the most successful horses on the track may not have hit the highest price bracket at Newmarket, but they can turn up trumps in the final reckoning.

There are a vast number of racing enthusiasts who are not often present on the course except at their nearest meeting – radio and television have brought thousands of fans and have made certain horses and the places associated with them every-day household words. Names like Longchamps — home of the French classic race, Le Prix de l'Arc de Triomphe; Epsom, where the Derby, the blue riband of the racing world, is run every year in June; Aintree, home of the world's greatest steeplechase; Aqueduct on Long Island, New York, and Churchill Downs, and finally Kentucky, venue for the great Kentucky Derby, are all well-known to many millions of people. Similarly, names of horses come to the fore through the mass media. Ribot and Man o'War, Nijinsky and Arkle are names that crop up time and again. These horses have become idols in their time, so popular that people will pay ridiculous sums for shoes worn by the horse in question. Eventually the popularity of some reach pop-star proportions and they have to be protected from their fans, who are often keen to obtain souvenirs, such as hairs from their favourite's tail.

Statues are erected in memory of these great horses. Hyperion and Chamossaire stand for ever at the centre of English racing, and their life-size models are to be seen at Newmarket, while Gladiateur guards the entrance to Longchamps. Similarly Man o'War lives on at Fayette County near Lexington in the heart of American racing country, Kentucky. China models are cast of the top favourites, pictures are painted and reproduced in thousands for the fans. You can now decorate your home with portraits of Mill Reef, Golden Miller and Sir Ivor; or with a porcelain model of your favourite steeplechaser, flat racer or show jumper. Racing in England takes place on the springy green turf as it does in Australia, but this is not always the case in other parts of the world. Aqueduct has a dirt track, Laurel Park has both grass and dirt

tracks though in the main racing in America takes place on dirt tracks.

It is not only the horses and places that become household names — jockeys and trainers are equally popular, such as the legendary Fred Archer, or Sir Gordon Richards, now a highly successful trainer, or Scobie Breasley, an Australian who did much of his race-riding in Britain. Others are Lester Piggot, who still stands unrivalled at the top of his profession, Yves Saint Martin, Eddie Arcaro and William Shoemaker of America. And don't forget the steeplechase jockeys, Arkle's partner, Pat Taafe, and Tommy Smith who came to England with Jay Trump from America and won the Grand National in 1965. Then there is Fred Winter, who won the French steeplechase on Mandarin with a broken bit, his only remaining control being the reins round the horse's neck.

These and many more are given film star treatment during their careers, but it is not all glamour. They have all worked long and hard and patiently to perfect their skill and that of their horses and have often had to wait for their successes. There is also a great deal of effort put in behind the scenes by the faithful stable lads and grooms, which goes unnoticed by the general public, but which is essential to any success. And the horses work hard too — the immortal Arkle won over £75,000 for his owner, having cost 1,150 guineas as a youngster at the Dublin Sales. But to win this huge sum steeplechasing, Arkle had to gallop almost 100 miles and jump some 600 fences and hurdles. In contrast, a three year old colt in the Derby can earn nearly as much by running twelve furlongs on the flat and winning this English Classic.

**Previous page: Left** Out of the stalls and they're off! The start of France's premier race, the Prix de l'Arc de Triomphe. Run at Lougchamps on the outskirts of Paris, this race attracts the best racehorses in Europe.

**Right** A portrait of Mill Reef with Geoff Lewis up. Owned by Paul Mellon, though English trained, he was the outstanding race horse of 1971 winning the Eclipse stakes, the Derby, the Prix de l'Arc de Triomphe, and the King George VI and Queen Elizabeth Stakes.

**Top left** The great Nijinsky, one of the outstanding horses of the 1970s, and maybe of all time. This Canadian bred, Irish-trained colt caught the public's imagination with his star-like quality during his racing career. Only the twelfth horse in 161 years to win the 'Triple Crown', which includes the 2000 guineas, the Derby and the St Leger, Nijinsky's ancestry can be traced back to one of the all-time greats in the racing world – Lord Derby's Hyperion. Ridden by champion jockey, Lester Piggot, he is seen here returning to the winner's enclosure at Ascot after his victory in the King George VI and Queen Elizabeth Stakes.

**Centre left** The field rounding Tattenham corner at Epsom.

**Bottom left** The ten minutes before a race are often more important than the race itself, as those who have backed a horse anxiously watch to see if their favourite is looking fit, or to examine the going and study the changing odds. One's earlier decision to back a horse which has been based on breeding, form and the jockey booked to ride may suddenly be reversed as one sees the rest of the field walking round the paddock. The jockeys mount and positively the last chance to judge the animals and change one's mind is when they canter down to the start. Here Tribal Chief and Joe Mercer go down to the start at Windsor Great Park.

**Right** Racehorses in the northern territory of Australia set out from the paddock for the start of a race at Brunette Downs. The racing will be on a sandy track presenting a very different picture from the English racing scene on the green turf. Australia is one of the most successful racing nations in the world and several speed records have been set up at the Randwick Racecourse in Sydney.

**Top left** A close finish as the end wire comes up at Aqueduct. These modern race jockeys owe their inheritance of the 'crouch' seat to James Todhunter Sloan ('Tod Sloan'). He was an American jockey who in 1897 brought the now familiar forward seat from America to the British Isles. He showed that by crouching forward with very short leathers, wind-resistance could be reduced and a faster speed would therefore result.

**Centre left** The post parade at Aqueduct, the racecourse on Long Island, New York. These colourful parades are a popular and eye-catching feature of American race tracks. The runners are escorted to the post by red-jacketed outriders and grooms.

**Bottom left** Neck and neck these pacers vie for position in an exciting contest. A major racing event on the North American continent, this sport does not attract very much attention in the British Isles, but is popular in Australia and New Zealand as well as several European countries.

**Right** A trainer and his string out at exercise in mid-winter. Whatever the weather, racehorses must be exercised. Often it is only walking, which is one of the best paces for getting a horse fit, combined with the occasional trot and short sharp burst at a faster speed, known as a 'pipe-opener'. Warmly rugged-up they will leave their stable yard in the early morning for their prescribed amount of exercise.

**Top left** A gaily coloured field passing the stands at Ascot. The Royal Ascot meeting is one of the most popular in the country and the women who go to the members enclosure are notorious for vying with each other over the size, colour and brilliance of their hats.

**Bottom left** The field take the water jump at Aintree during the Grand National. Any horse that runs in this race has to be supremely strong and fit to survive the gruelling course.

**Right** The much loved Arkle, only unplaced once in seventy races, thirty-five of which he won, proved himself beyond all doubt to be a truly great steeplechaser. He had three Cheltenham Gold Cups to his credit, the Irish Grand National, the King George VI Chase, the Henessy Gold Cup (twice) and many other top class victories too numerous to mention. These achievements tell their own story. Owned by Anne, Duchess of Westminster, Arkle was retired from racing as a result of his tragic accident at Kempton Park in 1966 when he broke his pedal bone. For almost two years, owner and trainer and all his supporters waited patiently to see if he would run again. Courageously, his owner took the unenviable decision that Arkle should never race again. This was a truly great horse with an unquenchable spirit and a desire to win at all costs. He loved the admiration of his followers and was a tremendous showman whenever he appeared in public. His reception at the Horse of the Year Show when he appeared in the Personalities Parade was similar to that accorded to a member of Royalty, and he enjoyed every minute of it.

**Right** The field taken during the Langley Handicap Hurdle Race at Windsor and (**Left**) a study of one of the horses as he takes off through a gap.

**Bottom left** Spanish Steps – a likely contender for the Cheltenham Gold Cup in 1972 seen here in the Gainsborough Chase at Sandown Park.

**Below** Two steeplechasers race against each other as they come in to land after the last fence.

# Horses on Show

Whether on ceremonial duty in honour of a State visit or performing the intricate movements of the *haute école* at the Spanish Riding School in Vienna, many horses spend a great deal of their lives on show under the gaze of the public all over the world. These glamorous horses include the ceremonial horses from the Royal stables in London and Copenhagen, Stockholm and Teheran, the show jumpers and Three Day Eventers, the world class polo ponies, hunt horses, show ponies, rodeo ponies and many more. For these, life moves at a faster pace and is more luxurious, though they are nearly all very highly trained and represent some of the most intelligent of their race. They all have their place in the equine world but it is those on show who receive the admiration of the public.

On the American continent several specialized breeds were developed by the early colonials which are now mainly show horses, although the Quarter Horse is also a good hard working animal not necessarily 'showy'. It is perhaps the best known of the American breeds as it has spread far and wide because of its excellent qualities and great versatility. Its name comes from the quarter mile races for which the horses were bred about three hundred years ago, and they make expert cow ponies and rodeo horses. In the latter

capacity they shine in the ring before crowds of thousands. Two stylish parade horses are the American Saddlehorse and the Tennessee Walking Horse, both of which are known for their easy gaits, while the outstanding harness racer in the world today is the American Standardbred which can be either a trotter or a pacer and possesses a lot of Thoroughbred blood.

The five main rodeo events, bareback riding, saddle bronc riding, bull riding, calf roping and steer wrestling all originate from the cowboy's everyday tasks on the ranch. From the earliest days in the west, when two or three cowboys would bet on each others' skill in the main street of their home town, the rodeo has grown to the large scale sport of today that can be seen all over the North American Continent. The professional riders can earn large sums of money and have attained a very high standard of skill and speed in all the events. The term rodeo did not come into use until the 1920s but the events were popular sports in the late nineteenth century.

Some of the biggest events attract visitors from all over the continent and overseas, who come to watch the cowboy pit his skills against his rival as well as against the broncs and bulls chosen to test his nerve and ability. The California Rodeo at

Salinas runs for four days and includes a daily parade down Main Street of over 1,000 horses and riders all decked out in authentic western costume. Ogden in Utah offers the thrills and spills of a pony express race and a goat-tying match. Cheyenne, as its name implies, boasts a tribal dance demonstration by Sioux Indians and a parade of horse-drawn vehicles unequalled anywhere in the world. But surely the crown must go to the ten day Calgary Stampede which combines the usual attractions of rodeo with a food fair, an exhibition of livestock, commercial exhibits and square dancing in the streets. The Stampede Parade lasts about two hours in downtown Calgary as all the participants parade in their magnificent costumes.

Horses which are perhaps the most impressive and beautiful on show are the grey Lippizaner stallions of the Spanish Riding School of Vienna. The School is renowned for having the most highly skilled riders and perfectly trained horses in the world, and their displays are world famous. It was founded in the eighteenth century and was named after the horses which are of Spanish origin, though it has always been situated in Vienna. The Lippizaners, horses of great intelligence, beauty and stamina, are specially bred at their stud in Piber, Austria, and all come from five families. Only the stallions are taken for the long and complex training, which begins after years of very careful breaking in and the normal training that most good riding horses undergo. They then learn all the special manoeuvres for which they are famous; the volte, which is the execution of very small circles, the Pesade, a turn on the haunches; Levade, Piaffe, Passage and so on. Perhaps the most spectacular is the Capriole when the horse springs high in the air and then when he reaches his highest point kicks out horizontally with his hind legs so that it seems as if he is flying.

The meet before a day's hunting is often a very attractive scene and

draws local spectators. The horses are always fit and well turned out, and usually excited at the thought of the chase ahead of them. The pink coats of the huntsmen and the shining leather and saddlery stand out above the shifting scene of people and hounds, which move like quicksilver around the whipper-in. Once the hounds have found there is no stopping the field as they swallow up hedge after hedge, providing a thrilling sight to those who are clever enough to follow close behind them. Although the interest in shows and jumping has increased enormously all over the world during the last ten years, the excitement of jumping unknown obstacles at speed and in company cannot be equalled in the artificial atmosphere of the show jumping arena. Not even riding a cross country course at a Three Day Event can equal the devil-may-care attitude of the hunter in pursuit of his quarry.

Another highly trained animal that has many eyes upon him is the polo pony. Polo is the oldest of the equestrian games, and is one of the most thrilling forms of organized mounted sport. It is a very exciting game to watch and is even more exciting to play, demanding immense skill and strength always at top speeds, all of which only comes after years of practice. The ponies are very valuable and also need much patient schooling and practice, and polo is thus a very expensive pastime.

Next time you go to a show or to the meet of the local hunt or maybe a polo match, spare a thought for the work that goes on behind the scenes in order to produce the supremely fit and well-trained animals that you are privileged to watch. There are countless grooms who devote their lives to the welfare of the horses in their charge and often spend all their time tending to a sick or injured animal when they should be off-duty or catching up on their sleep. Girls who are employed in the big hunting stables begin their day at crack of dawn to prepare their charges and then have to cope with dirty and exhausted horses when they return at night after an arduous day's hunting.

**Previous page: Left** A very smart coach and four on the marathon stage in Richmond Park. There has been a tremendous increase in the interest in driving in Great Britain and in the USA, and many people are starting to collect gigs and carriages to drive round the countryside behind a keen little pony or a stylish horse.

**Right** Once a year the London Harness Horse Society organizes the London Harness Horse Parade when both light and heavy trade turnouts gather in Regent's Park in London. Beautifully turned out, the exhibits are presented with awards and then parade around the Inner Circle in the Park. This magnificent pair of black Shires have stopped for a quick snack out of their nosebags. These bags are carried during working hours so that there is no necessity to return to the stables during the day. Lunch can then be taken anywhere en route while the driver enjoys his own meal, probably in the nearest pub, while his team munch happily through their rations.

———————

**Below** Not much can be seen of these handsome Shires underneath their beautifully decorated harness, which is the traditional finery of plumes, ribbons, straws and the shining horse brasses. Their owners compete not only to plough the straightest furrow with their team, but also to produce the most splendid animals. Interest in breeding Shires, Suffolk Punches, and Clydesdales is growing both in Britain and America, and of course the magnificent sight of a team decked out in full regalia is very popular.

**Right** Both pony and rider must be highly skilled to play the fast-moving and dangerous game of polo. Here the rider sits high in the saddle as he swings for the ball. Prince Philip, a keen player, has had to retire from the game due to a painful injury.

The Lippizaner stallions of the Spanish Riding School of Vienna photographed during one of their spectacular displays in the ring which adjoins the Imperial Palace.

**Previous page: Left** The Pesade perfectly performed. This movement is learned first of all from a loose rein with no rider, and much of the training is accomplished when the horse is tethered lightly between two posts about four feet apart.
**Right** The Courbette, a movement once performed in battle. The horse balances on his hind legs and then with deeply bent hocks leaves the ground altogether in one perfectly controlled movement.

---

**Left** The Passage, which is a slowly forward-moving Piaffe and can be seen performed by experts in England. It is like a slow and graceful trot, very dignified and regular.

**Below** The Spanish Trot performed on the diagonal against the magnificent renaissance architecture of the school.

**Right** Members of the School entering the ring for the Quadrille. Dressed in their traditional uniform of black bicorn, tail coat, dazzling white breeches and shining top boots, they salute the portrait of their founder, and then sometimes ride in single file right into the main visitors' box and canter round the somewhat startled guests in a tight circle before starting the display.

**Left** From the moment that the chute opens and the bronc bursts out into the open the buster's trial begins. The requisite eight seconds he must stay aboard in the bare back class must seem like a lifetime, and some broncs become famous for their ability to unfailingly land their rider on the ground. In saddle bronc riding the requisite time is ten seconds and in both one hand has to be left free and held high above the horse. The bronc (**below**) would appear to have achieved his ambition and rid himself of his buster.

**Right** The Old Surrey and Burstow hounds at the meet, together with the hunt staff. It is estimated that 50,000 mounted followers hunt every week in Britain. Foxhunting is also extremely popular in America, mainly in Virginia where some fine packs (with a preponderance of English blood lines) are to be found. Where there is a shortage of foxes, or none at all, the hunt follows a drag, or man-made trail as a substitute. It is never quite the same as fox hunting, when the excitement enables one to jump further and faster than ever before. The hunting field provides the ideal schooling ground for a young horse, whether he is destined for the eventing world, show jumping or steeplechasing.

**Above** Rodeos take place where the modern cowboy can compete against his fellow workers to show off his and his mount's skill in the arena. Roping calves, which forms a major part of his everyday work, is one of the many organized events together with bull-dogging, cutting out, bronco-busting and driving waggon teams at breakneck speed. Complete co-ordination between horse and rider is essential if a calf is to be roped successfully. As soon as the lassoo has found its mark the horse will stop short and take the weight of the calf as the rope is firmly attached to saddle. The cowboy then leaps to the ground and ties the calf securely.

**Left** For a week in the spring the Spanish town of Seville is given over to the famous Seville April Fair, at which business is essentially still the selling and buying of horses. Fiesta time is the signal for the handsome horsemen to parade along the streets of Seville on their beautiful Carthusian and Arab horses, sometimes unaccompanied, and at other times carrying girls dressed in their exquisite dresses *a crupa* behind them. With the gaily decorated streets, Seville offers one of the most splendid sights to be found anywhere in the world.

**Right** Heavy horses are naturally not seen nearly so much as they used to be now that their work can be done by machine. However, they are still used in the forests of Canada and Scotland and very occasionally for ploughing in hilly country, and the various different breeds are still being bred by enthusiasts. This is a Shire horse on parade at a show.

**Left** The American Saddlebred is a five-gaited horse now bred almost exclusively for the show ring. His bearing is outstanding and the very high arched head carriage is characteristic as is the high tail carriage.

**Below** Two heavy horses visiting the blacksmith before going on parade.

**Right** 'The horse first, and then yourself'. One of the Canadian 'Mounties' (Royal Canadian Mounted Police) puts the finishing touches to his equipment after he has prepared his mount before going on parade. Established in 1871 to help settle the west, they are still famous for their wonderful mounted nusical rides.

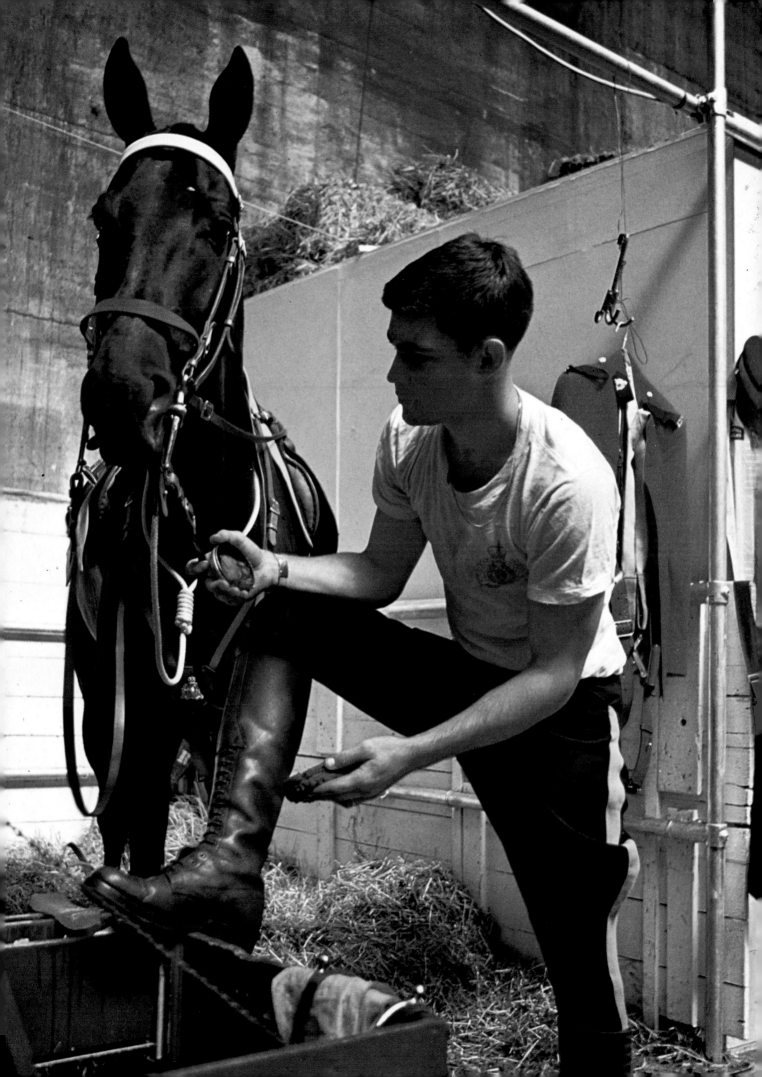

**Right** The Royal Horse Guards, or 'The Blues' as they are popularly known, make up the Household cavalry together with the Life Guards. Recently amalgamated with the Royal Dragoons, they are now more often known as 'The Blues and Royals'. Their uniform differs form the well-known Life Guards (**Left**) in that they have red plumes, blue tunics and black sheepskins on their saddles. The Household Cavalry obtain their handsome black horses from Ireland as three and four year olds and except for the State Trumpeters, who ride grey horses, and the drum horses who are piebald or skewbald, all the troop horses are black.

**Below** The drum horses of the Household Cavalry have to be exceptionally strong to carry the weight of the huge silver drums for long periods. Here the men are dressed in their gold state coats and velvet caps originating from the time of Charles II. This uniform is worn only in the presence of royalty. During the summer, the Household Cavalry makes the journey down to Pirbright in Surrey for a period under canvas and a chance for the horses (and the troopers) to stretch their legs on the soft turf of the commons after the hard tarmac of the London streets. Troop horses also compete successfully in show jumping and eventing during the summer season and some lucky ones are based in the centre of the hunting country in Leicestershire for the winter season.

# Ponies

The difference between horses and ponies is often thought to be purely one of size, however not only does the size limit for a pony vary, but there are other equally important differences between them. The normal height limit of a show pony is 14 to 14.2 hands, though the National Pony Society in Britain has accepted animals up to 15.2 hands in height for breeding purposes. Moreover, the beautiful Arabian is classified as a horse the world over, and they are often well below 14 hands, so no hard and fast line can be drawn. It is in temperament, character and general hardiness that ponies differ from horses. They have a compact body, small, sharp pricked ears and usually a rougher coat than a horse, and a definite pony expression which is difficult to describe though instantly recognizable. They can fend for themselves, are surefooted and clever at getting out of awkward corners. On the whole more intelligent than horses, they often have much more positive characters with more than just a dash of mischievousness, and are capable of giving great affection.

There are of course a vast number of ponies of unidentifiable ancestry and of no particular breed, the result of years of cross-breeding, but there are also plenty of specimens of the many different pony breeds that exist

throughout the world. On various islands and in specific parts of the world there are still herds of wild ponies roaming over moors all the year round; notable are the celebrated Carmargue ponies in southern France, the Shetland ponies that still thrive in the harsh conditions of their native islands, though vast numbers have now been bred in captivity and in warmer conditions to meet popular demand, the Chincoteaque ponies of the islands off the Virginian coast, and the Dartmoor and New Forest ponies.

The British Isles are endowed with a wealth of native breeds, and much of the world's high class pony stock is based upon them. Welsh Mountain ponies are much in demand in America and in South Africa, as they are generally considered to be the most beautiful and stylish of all ponies, having very neat heads much like those of the Arab horses. They also make ideal children's ponies, as do the Dartmoor and the New Forest ponies, all of which have their own particular characteristics. Many famous performers in the show ring and in Eventing can trace their ancestry back to these pony stocks, and indeed a good Eventing horse needs a drop of pony blood to give him the necessary wits and stamina to cope with the 'natural' fences in a cross country course.

Among other well-known breeds are the Haflinger of Austria, described as a 'Prince in front and a peasant behind', the spotted Appaloosas which are a recognized breed in America, and the Connemara ponies from Ireland.

There are few areas of the world that do not possess at least one native breed of horse or pony but the European continent has such a wide variety of ponies and horses that many other areas of the world have imported breeding stock from Europe in order to improve their standards. Ireland has always been a favourite hunting ground for riding horses and Great Britain has almost unlimited supplies of ponies, hunters and successful competition horses. It is still possible to pick up a bunch of unbroken New Forest ponies at the Beaulieu Road Sales in the New Forest for a reasonable price. But unbroken ponies need expert training and the novice should avoid the temptation of buying an unbroken pony cheaply.

Two of the most famous ponies in the history of the horse world were the South American Criollo ponies Mancha and Gato. These two incredibly tough little animals were the heroes of a fantastic ride of 13,000 miles from Buenos Aires to New York. This ride was undertaken by Aime Tschiffley in the 1920s to prove the stamina of the Criollo pony. The ponies were 15 and 16 years old when the journey began, it lasted two and a half years and the ponies both lived well into their thirties. The Criollo stands about 14 hands high and is usually dun in colour, but skewbalds and piebalds are often found. They have been imported to other parts of the world in large numbers to be trained as polo ponies.

Ponies are among the most rewarding of creatures for a family to possess, and give endless pleasure. However, they all need careful looking after and correct feeding and exercising so the responsibility of owning a pony must not be regarded lightly.

**Previous page: Left** As the thousands of holiday-makers travel to the west of England every summer, they can see the herds of Dartmoor ponies as their road winds over the wild expanse of moor. The Dartmoor pony is small, tough, sure-footed and ideal as a child's first pony. Endowed with a fine head carriage, good presence and an excellent front, he is a good breed to cross with a larger type to produce top class show ponies and horses. The Dartmoor lives the whole year round on the exposed moorland and is therefore very hardy.

**Right** Two New Forest youngsters at the Beaulieu Road sales on the edge of the New Forest. The New Forest pony has evolved from a mixture of blood and is the largest of the British native breeds, anything up to 14.2 hands being acceptable. He can therefore be termed a real family pony as he is quite capable of carrying lightweight adults. Their temperament is ideal for children and they are usually very quiet in traffic as they see plenty during their early life in the Forest. The New Forest pony is very sure-footed and hardy like all the British native breeds, and this is yet another point in his favour.

---

**Below** The semi-wild white ponies of the Carmargue in Southern France. The local farmers round them up periodically and brand them to keep an eye on their condition and numbers. Sometimes they break them in to help on the farm and act as cow ponies.

**Right** A smart, well turned out, part-Arab pony waiting to go for a ride.

**Above and left** This Gypsy pony is obviously one of the family, and has an old-time, smartly painted caravan to draw, though the actual process of linking the two together appears to cause a little difficulty. The true Romany gypsies were the traditional horse dealers of the world but now they are a vanishing race and the few that are left usually have motor vehicles of some kind.

**Right** A palomino pony half asleep in the sun. Ponies are sociable creatures and love to hang over a gate watching any goings on. If their grazing is isolated it is best for them to have company of some kind, either another pony or horse, and they can be turned out with a dairy herd or a flock of sheep.

# Acknowledgements

The publisher would like to thank the following individuals and organizations for their kind permission to reproduce the following pictures in this book:

American Saddle Horse Breeders Association, 62 top; The Appaloosa Horse Club Inc. USA, 30; Australian News & Information Bureau, 31 bottom; Barnaby's Picture Library, 66; Colour Library International, 29, 43, 62 bottom; C M Dixon, 5; Fox Photos, 42 top, 53; The Historical Picture Service, 4; Michael Holford, 6 bottom, 7, 19; Elizabeth Johnson, 38 top; Keystone Press Agency, 10, 13, 31 top, 38 bottom, 46, 47, 52, 68; Geoffrey Kinns, Associated Freelance Artists, 9 bottom, 21 bottom; Ed Lacey, 20, 21, 22, 23, 24, 25, 42 centre and bottom, 46 top, 48, 49; Colin Lofting, 60 top; London Express News & Feature Service, 40, 45; Daniel O'Keefe, 34 bottom, 35; Walter D Osborne, 36 top, 44 top and centre; Van Phillips, 8, 9 top, 64, 65; Paul Popper, 33; Peter Roberts, 16, 17, 32, 61, 63; W W Rouch & Co, 41; Spanish Riding School of Vienna, 54, 55, 56, 57; Spectrum Colour Library, 6 top, 11, 12, 14 top, 15, 18, 28, 36 bottom, 37, 39, 50, 51, 59, 60 bottom, 67, 70, 71; Syndication International, 26, 27; United States Trotting Association, 44 bottom; Barbara Woodhouse, 69; Adam Woolfitt, 34 top, 58.